Early Train

Acknowledgements

A number of these poems were published in the pamphlet *A Horse Called House* (smith | doorstop, 1997). *Early Train* won Second Prize in the Tabla Poetry Competition, 2001; 'Driving the Children' was longlisted for the Bridport Prize (Poetry) 2009; 'The Sudden Shower' won Third Prize in the Bridport Prize (Poetry) 1997; 'Food' was selected and published by the 2010 Ver Poetry Competition under the title 'Custard'; all have been subsequently re-drafted. 'Holidays', 'Lane' and 'On Learning a Poem by Peter Didsbury' were published in *The North*. 'Train Watching' was published by *Smiths Knoll*. The poems 'Photograph: Apple Pickers, 1981', 'The Sudden Shower', 'Tony', 'Coningsby in Constantinople', 'Early Train', 'A Short Piece of Choral Music' and 'Domestic' were all published in Spanish translation (by Katherine M. Hedeen and Víctor Rodríguez Núñez) in *La Otra* (Mexico) With thanks to Sara Beadle, Maura Dooley, Roz Goddard and members of The Poetry Business's Writing School 2010–2011.

Early Train
Jonathan Davidson

smith|doorstop

Published 2011 by
smith | doorstop Books
The Poetry Business
Bank Street Arts
32-40 Bank Street
Sheffield S1 2DS
www.poetrybusiness.co.uk

ISBN 978-1-906613-32-7

British Library Cataloguing-in-Publication Data.
A catalogue record for this book is available from the
British Library.

Typeset by Utter
Printed by Charlesworth, Wakefield
Cover design by Utter
Cover image: Pont-Melvez Station, Cote d'Armor, France
Author photo: Sara Beadle

smith | doorstop Books is a member of Inpress,
www.inpressbooks.co.uk. Distributed by Central Books Ltd.,
99 Wallis Road, London E9 5LN.

The Poetry Business gratefully acknowledges the help of
Arts Council England.

Supported by
ARTS COUNCIL
ENGLAND

Contents

For Margaret, Fred and Mollie

Food

Dad was the hunter-gatherer: rabbits hit by cars
on lonely roads, like burst hot water bottles;
he'd have them wrapped in *The Morning Star*,
saddle-bagged and stiffening.

Not to mention apples where they'd fallen
and where they'd not. And blackberries from both sides
of the fence, perfumed with petrol, bloomed
and tarnished by sunshine and by dust.

And still warm, greed-stupid pheasant-mannequins;
pigeons with broken necks, un-flighted, still;
dark eyed sloes; percussive hazelnuts, damsons,
and once, in a private wood, strawberries.

All to be plucked and gutted, stuffed or bottled,
hung up for days or put down for winter,
jammed into jars, by Mum,

who pickled onions, baked and decorated cakes,
kneaded the dough for pumice-hollow loaves;
stripped the hare's fur coat
with a single incision and a good tug.

When the marmalade pan was lifted off the heat,
she'd watch the sea settling like lava,
thick with stiff Castilian peel.

Waste not, want not.
Plums don't grow on trees.
Only a fool would refuse a gooseberry flan.

The Sudden Shower

Time tells. The day clouds over.
A sudden shower. Rain beating a path
to our childhood door.

She is typing in the bedroom.
Broken notes. The bell's ping.
Her hand driving the bar back

to where it belongs again
and again until the rain's
gravelly rattle sends us

flying up the garden path
to have wet washing stacked
on our arms, fist-fulls of pegs

stuffed in our pockets, always
the great haste to bring
the harvest home. What

she was typing is caught
half-in, half-out of being,
nearly naked. The clothes horse

is saddled-up, the gas fire
ticks and hisses, a dinner
is put in hand. We wait

for Dad's big soaking steps
to fill the kitchen, his voice
to clatter dishes. Her poem's

not completed, gone already.

Hide and Seek

Because we might be killed at any moment,
knocked down by a car or struck by lightning
or one of those sinister neighbours sent
to collect us from school; because we sing
along the pavements; because we are so
blind to dangers and will not, cannot, see
we like to hide. Our parents always know
but stride round the house inexplicably
failing to find us, until just before
we're due to set off; what sprung joy then
as we leap out! Except that time the door
closed, the key turned, we counted to ten
and ten again, the house emptied of sound,
and we were lost: unsure, undone, unfound.

The Cul de Sac

Next summer the silver birch will shimmer
in a cold breeze and the rose trees will turn
yellow and red.

Now a black car slips into a driveway:
the sweet thump thump of tyres
and the dead quiet when the engine cuts.

A cat drops from a shed.
A light snaps on and a door slams.
A gas fire is sparked into hissing heat.
Green or blue curtains close.

Breathless, a giddy child is danced in a front room.
When he is stopped he stares at the long mirror,
at the shiny picture of himself,
a hand raised in greeting and goodbye.

The Boy

We walk the lanes. Tucked into a corner
of country, they map the boundaries
that hold the fields and coppices and covers,
and catch the sunlight, refracting years.

The fibs and half-truths, lies and leadings-on
of small roads are a fabrication
and fabric of a history that's dumb
but deeper than dates, and goes further in.

Often a tree or stump of stone roots-up
a nodal point of intrigue, the chart
not telling the palpable truth, that livestock
grazed or were fetched-in near here, or that

a small boy lived at the track's end, or that
he disappeared one summer, happy or unhappy.

Goodbye

Goodbye to the smell of the rain on the tarmac
of the pavements of the cul-de-sacs and crescents
of childhood, and corner-shops with proprietors
with print-stained fingers.

Goodbye to raindrops in hoops of chain-link fences
at the bottoms of gardens that backed onto grounds
of schools, and the poplar trees patrolling the lengths
with un-climbable trunks.

Goodbye to the cat in the sun and the sunhat left
in the deckchair's sag by a parent called inside
by a trimphone, in a hall whose echoing gloom
was chilly and flustered.

Goodbye to the gunfire and clamouring chatter
of the hand-pushed lawnmower, leaving its shadow
on the nap of a lawn long ago laid, and goodbye
to the dead man pushing it.

Holidays

Washing in the mill race;
water like fire, freezing,
and the stones worn by it.

Each day we climbed up
through waves of bracken
or fern, finding outcrops

of igneous rocks, settled
into knuckles, the giant
we let sleep. When rain

rolled north we rode through
the floods past the cars,
towards the hill standing

proudly up from the levels.
To look from there was
to see our lives before us,

but later that afternoon
found us on the train, headed
home, flushed with the sun

caught on our faces and
our arms, our muscles a little
more prominent, one less

holiday ahead of us, one
more set of maps marked
with the thick pencil lines.

Early Train

Leaving the house in half-dark, I am going
without goodbye, pulling the front door shut

with a muffled clunk. During the night,
at two and then at three o'clock, the four

and then the six year old had clambered up
into our narrow bed. We'd all slept sound

in the same moonlight from the street lamp
marooned across the bay from our harbour,

and the sea of leaves that turned in the trees
was a fierce squall that filled our dreaming.

As the night went out, scouring temporary
channels in the sand, we would, one by one,

wake up. I was the first, and before I left
to cycle to the station, I took a photo

of the three of them, in the five-thirty light,
to remember the lie of their bodies becalmed,

their faces and voices, their words and replies
washed up on the further shore, to remember

what it was we became when we lived together.

The Day

Tired from the day, I sit pretending to read.
You're here too, turning page after page with the intensity
of the transported spirit.

Outside, our children and a pack of others are singing and shouting.
We ignore them, or try to.

Every now and then we pick up a note of distress, and we pause –
you in your reading, me in my pretending –
to convince ourselves that no one's hurt
or about to be.

It's always nothing.

They know we're here so they can ignore us
just as we can't block out
the sounds of them.

Eventually we stop hearing their voices:
there is a neat silence and all of them, ours included,
will have been hauled off to bed
complaining.

The day has ended.

Driving the Children

We've driven through a gazetteer
of places of interest, thousands of miles
with the children asleep in the back.

They woke to sun on the last afternoon
of a wet holiday. They stirred as we rolled
and pitched through seasonal road works.

When we debated happiness and how to get it,
they nodded off. And when we talked
about how we loved them, they snored.

Despite our eyes aching in Midland fog,
despite the needle hovering on empty,
and the three point turn on the bypass,

they trusted us to bring them safely home,
to lift them from their dreams and carry them
bodily, suddenly heavy, up the front steps

into the house, and up the stairs to their beds.

Family Traits: An Explanation

Our kids are just like us, in equal measure.

The good in them, you are suggesting, comes from your line:
a love of manners; an interest in study, especially
homework, especially in the holidays, especially Maths and French;
a desire to please, particularly grown-ups;
liking to share –
all these are bred from your stock.

My lineage, you maintain, is a pudding of a different flavour.
From me they get, it turns out, loafing;
giving back as good as they get; going too far;
not going far enough;
a high opinion of themselves;
a low opinion of others;
being visibly bored by your friends and relatives;
fecklessness, foolishness, fickleness;
resorting to taunts and chuntering;
taking the huff and sulking on a celestial scale;
saying they'll do things and then never doing them,
except to please themselves.

These traits are marked with the indelible ink
of goods stolen from the back seat
of my ancestral saloon.

Our kids are just like us, in equal measure.

Sketch of my Father

I see you at a distance, complete,
your compact figure wheeling a bike,
one slight hand only on the handlebars,
or else pulling the pedals up a hill,
fighting the gradient. You are not angry
but some people have unnerved or even
disappointed you and now the days
are oddly shaped, the days fall over
their many selves to bring you back
to a Welsh field in wartime
and your child-self singing as you hacked
at bracken or watched the cows home.
You had a valley and a small mountain
to climb. And you had a boy's lifetime.

Song and Dance

Not able to remember the words
to a song but keen to sing and dance,
you take to the floor in our front room
between the sofa and occasional table.

You dance the jig or waltz or quick step
of a man who has come back from the dead
and haunts himself with his dancing days
after the war when he sang to overcome

a stammer. So now you sing and dance
while the kids fight over the remote,
desperate to watch anything on telly.
You stop. Take a bow. We turn the talk

to return trains and how you shouldn't
miss catching yours home. It's about *time* -
getting somewhere on it, not wasting it,
keeping to it; the best, the next, the last.

Dead to the World

Dead to the world you'd say you were,
with the cat asleep too, on your belly,
and the front room curtains twitching

in a draught. It's early evening
and you're resting after work,
your bike in the shed, your boots stood
[handwritten: standing !]

in the kitchen and the sun still
filling in the last of the shadows
around this house and the others.

Now the factory is fourteen miles
of indifferent road away. Its vapour
hangs over spires and meadows,

tarnishes the verges with fumes
and lets out an occasional roar,
which you hear as you sleep

with the cat sailing the solid swell
of breath in your lungs, till tea-time,
or whatever else, disturbs you.

Back from the Dead

I
You lay like an Egyptian prince or a Greek king,
still as marble or the moon.
But you were alive.

Around your head,
with its halo of beard and hair and stiff pillows,
the unsleeping monitors blinked;
blood pulled through ventricles,
a shuffle of breath forced open your lungs.

A life eclipsed not extinguished.

II
You'd never been a king or prince or even a courtier,
only a man cycling to work past private orchards,
crossing river bridges under cold clouds.

But the days had clambered over one another,
and the months had gone on ahead;
and the years didn't look forward.

III
Come back to us and if you do
the kingdom, the country, its fields and parks, estates
and railways, road signs and contra flows, the drains
and ditches, flood plains and tidal causeways,
the stands and hangers, will be yours,

the sky and the earth beneath it,
the seas and oceans,
will be yours.

The Flowers

Held upright, or just about,
with twine or insulation tape,
some still in their cellophane,
or in a jam-jar of water;

bought from roadside stalls
or petrol stations en route or cut
from gardens the morning after
by relatives or friends.

There are messages too:
heartfelt in felt-tip capitals
or done by a child in crayon
or a line of verse typed-up.

They are often seen on bridges
spanning motorways, the stems
wilting but unable to collapse;
traffic moving freely beneath.

Tony
i.m. A.W.

I'm reconciling a bank account, thinking of you.
A thousand little contracts keep me in the black.
I've found things in my garage I didn't know
were there. It's not that I needed or loved you
more than was necessary. Every transaction
in the world is linked to every other; firmer
than faith or hope, we are held by numbers.
You had years left, then how many months,
then the days, which went. The minutes: dust.
In the garage looking for something or other,
I find you in the charnel darkness, in the chaos
and disorder, the lost stuff. I am un-reconciled.

In Praise of Apples
for Dr Barrie Juniper

Out of the fruit forests of Tien Shan
Carried by horse and bear, by man

Kind and man unkind, they came,
The sweet apples, bearing the name

Of love, desire, betrayal, death.
Aphrodisiac; cleanser of breath,

Opener of bowels, universal cure,
A womb around a foetal core,

Flesh rattling with cyanide pips,
Firm promise for the lover's lips.

They store the sunlight that we lost,
They weather forty nights of frost

And carry stories, each given name
A little history that came

With nimble fingered grafting knife,
The fatal cut creating life.

And though a bite may be the last
You take, the apple empire's vast

And catalogued varieties
Of tended and untended trees

Still hold, sway.

Photograph: Apple Pickers, 1981

Small orchard and apple pickers.
Four young people from the town,
six village women and one old man,
gardener, memory of how things were,
and the owner, Miss Balcombe,
unmarried mother of the trees.

I am stood by a wheelbarrow.
One girl is sat in it, lost in light,
her brown cords tight-fitting like bark.
The village women link arms.
The old man holds a spade.
Miss Balcombe smiles
her crab-apple smile.

And behind us, the good trees:
Laxton's, Bramley's, a Wyken Pippin.
Full blown leaves rattle in a North Berkshire gale,
thick roots penetrate rich loam, reach into clay,
hold themselves steady for the season.

I went back last year: they had gone,
the apple trees, the people.

On Learning a Poem by Peter Didsbury

I am learning a poem by Peter Didsbury,
speaking it to the apple-crisp morning while walking
the knife-narrow lane.

I'm using the 'image' method, linking each line
to an object or two, to anchor the words
in the stream of my mind.

Things are not going well; the poem, *Cider Story*,
is not cushion-stuffed with images and lots
of the language is opaque

and will not be still but keeps drifting off towards
the shallows of my consciousness
where the ducks are feeding.

There are no ducks in *Cider Story*, although two
have just cut the sky with their urgent flight.
And now a single hare sits up

in a field and looks at me in much the same way
I imagine Peter Didsbury would, although
neither of them are in the poem.

And then a deer springs rhythmically across my path
into a thicket: his publishers, surely,
astonished at my nerve.

And here comes a red and yellow low-loader loaded
with oblong portable public conveniences
bowling along the lane

heedless of my health and welfare, unaware
that I am trying to learn a poem by heart.
Then the black dog appears.

Then the white cat. Then the sound of the lapwing
and then the lapwing itself and by the time I enter
the neighbourhood watch area

I've barely half a stanza learned and images enough
to cobble courtyards with should I be of a mind
to do so, which I am.

Official Visit: Gods and Goddesses
i.m. The United Kingdom 2010 – 2015

Stepping down from gilded conveyances,
a small party of Gods and Goddesses –
ancient but modern – and a cherub
or two for recreation, observe their first
purgatorial diorama or tableau, enacted
for their delight by unwitting fools.

The Gods and Goddesses adjust their dress
and hold themselves still for the cameras,
glad of attention even from morons,
and then chat about the weather
and the awful smell of mortality.

This was not how they imagined Earth,
hardly a paradise, shocking really
when they consider the cost of keeping
so many of the beautiful animals alive
and ready for work.

*"Is this what we are obliged to watch over?
I had as soon observe my own latrine
as it pongs in the heavenly sunshine."*

*"But they enjoy it, that's what's important.
Their howls of pleasure are quite charming.
Now, could I tempt you to another cherub?"*

The Sultan's Locomotive
for Peter Didsbury

Hard to credit that they should lose a locomotive:
a hundred tonnes of stamp and temper,
of pitch and yaw; vaulter of rivers,
breaster of inclines; a lion, lost.

Not *lost* exactly: impacted in sand, driver and fireman
flung from their swaying daydreams, lucky
to be alive. A day's work buries their shame;
let the *shamal* winds do the rest.

It's still there, a desert curiosity, its ribs of steel
furred with rust. The crew are long gone,
fled the country, but their ridiculous story
moves on slowly, holds fast.

Jennings and Darbishire
i.m. Anthony Buckeridge

Both of you should be rotten with class hatred,
one father in the civil service, the other called
to the Ministry, funds perhaps a little stretched,
but you're courteous to everyone, assuming
adults to be past comprehension, mad as bats
but often jolly decent. Masters get into frantic
bates over your *laissez-faire* attitude to French.
Your interest in which of Harold's eyes took
the arrow is seen as blind cheek. Imagining
a wild west adventure, your scrapes are local.
The future is cricket against Bracebridge School,
on Saturday, to be won by a wicket. A Postal Order
from an Aunt means a slap-up feast of sausages
and sardines and sponge cake. You live your days
in a socialist utopia within a feudal construct.
The world is always righted before the end of term.
The sky fills with unreported horrors, ash clouds
blow over cities, and while the age's sirens sound
the stones of Linbury Court Preparatory School soak up
the cheerful late September sun, and two boys, known
only by their surnames, are friends beyond words.

Anthony Buckeridge (1912 – 2004) is best known for his series of novels
featuring schoolboys Jennings and Darbishire.

Cyclists

They come into view, in small groups
or ones and twos, down absent-minded lanes
sewn into hedges of flowering hawthorn,
older than England. Uphill they stand up
to race to the summit or sit back and pull
slowly until a new horizon settles in place.
On Roman roads they ride in formation,
chevroned into a stiff breeze, a peleton
poised for glory and the *maillot jeune*.

On good days the miles fall away; tea
brewed strong in the pot at each stop,
a hare glimpsed prancing in a March field,
a canal funnelling through the open lock,
and the roads well surfaced. On bad days
the rain runs down their necks and backs,
the tarmac's treacherous and the puddles
hide pot-holes while the hills are higher
than they should be and last for longer.

Quietly they go, around a sudden corner
or over the brow; quietly as the heron
moving itself across a modest estuary,
beating its wings into a cloudy sunset.
Then they tuck in for the final miles,
legs pushing, pedals turning, eyes fixed
on the next landmark: a three arch bridge,
a castle ruin with two keeps, a town sign:
heading for home, home heads for them.

The Long Climb

That was the day of the long climb and the quick
descent, just touching the brakes on the corners,
taking risks; but I got down safely. And I stood
for a minute or two, the bike leant against the brick
wall of the tea-shop to know what stillness was, to
catch my breath a bit. *I'll have a pot of tea please
and cheese on toast and some toast and a slice
of matrimony cake and a fruit scone. Thank you.*

And for that time I sat in the window checking
the map for the route home, I didn't know how
I would feel twenty years later, with those miles
in my muscles and the high passes stormed
and the tidal causeways crossed and re-crossed
and all the little roads leading to you;
but I did know, even then, that I had to get back,
never mind how tired I was. *Lovely. Thank you.*

Hetchins, Rotrax, Mercian

Makers of bespoke steel frames
for bicycles, a 19th Century art
carried out in backstreet lock-ups
or units in industrial zones.
There's craft in Hetchins' curly stays
or Rotrax's modest lugwork
or the barber's pole paintwork
of the Mercian tourer. And those
who ride them out on inclement
Sunday mornings through winters
or for a quick spin after work
along the old Welsh road or past
the deserted villages, or away
for months at a time, storming
the scorching Pyrenean passes,
they do not remain unmoved
by the spring and the balance
inherent in the steel triangles
but will not unduly eulogise
such simple, solemn genius.

Tenor Recorder

Rather breathy, throaty tenor recorder,
I had sooner you than ten thousand years
Of plangent, priapic guitar or the endless
Orgasm of the violin or his boastful pal,
The cello, or any of their libidinous family.

No, I want the plain bore of pushed air
And its shuddering tunnel of lost, deciduous
Voices, almost always about to peter out
Or collapse back into silence. Tenor recorder:
My hard heart, my wasted soul, my hollow life.

Famous Last Words

I
What could possibly go wrong? Where
in the Highway Code does it forbid
the wearing of deep sea diving suits?

II
Having thought it through I think our best
course of action is to wake the pilot
with a breath of fresh air. Here, let me …

III
One little match, just so we can find
our way out of this explosives factory
in which we strangely find ourselves.

IV
Well, being tied to a railway line is harsh
but if you think our relationship needs
a little give and take … Oh, you've gone.

V
Shall we split the atom like I suggested,
then we can both have half and enough light
to see us home from the laboratory?

Train Watching

With half an hour to kill he watches trains:
he wants to feel the pull as they pass through
at speed, so close to him, so many tonnes,
containerised, close-coupled, simple, true
to their natures. Coal hoppers, oil tankers,
an express taking the curve like a toy
pushed by a boy across a kitchen floor
while mum makes tea; the little tracks annoy
his father home from work, but for the moment
they keep him quiet. Quiet's what they notice
first off, years later, when his time is spent
no longer watching trains. The transport police
suggest he tripped and fell, but cannot say
what brought him to the platform edge that day.

The Train Crash

It was beautiful;
a small shrug of a shoulder,
a nudge of coincidence,
a table-top knocked in passing.

Someone was to blame but that didn't matter;
the crash had spoken and it had said
metal will tear at metal, flesh too.

We lit the scene and measured, counted.
How many is right for a crash of this magnitude?
Can we untie these knots of lives?
Where are the real tragedies?

Some stood in awe or surrender.
What had taken so long to create,
our poly-tunnelled faith in movement,
had withered with the blast of impact.

Then it was a nice day; the sheep
grumbled at the grass on the hillside,
a kingfisher plucked a fish
from the shallow river.

Lane

Cut into slabs of sandstone,
a drift of dead leaves lap
at its edges. To walk or cycle
down it is to enter the mind
of the pilgrim, the dark
striations are the claw marks
of good intentions and where
we are journeying will be
hot though the bosky shadows
make this lane cold. To rise
out of the sunken way, with
muscles aching from standing
on the pedals for leverage or
the heels' tendons stretched
and released in energetic
walking is to see the light
of days, of all our days, come
up into a plain horizon. And
suddenly we are out and on
top of the hill, with fields
and a nearby motorway
lying all around us and we
are unreasonably happy.

Coningsby at Constantinople

He lifts his face from the lap of Mahomet's daughter
and thinks of buttercups and winterbournes
and the tight hedged lanes of his native country
and cattle grazing on short, wet grass.

Her inarticulate cries were the voices
of the common birds of England, a crow,
a jackdaw, a second jackdaw, a flock of geese
high in the Salopian sky, in flight to heaven.

Later, she reads him a treatise on astrology,
how the earth curves and the moon moves.
He answers, endearingly, in squawks and whoops;
his tongue is not her own but she knows it.

Then, she prays for the symmetry of desire
as he dances and his feet describe her
in languages, his arms like little wings,
his feathers lifting in the desert air.

Humfrey Coningsby (1567 – 1610) was born at Neen Sollars in
Shropshire. In the later years of his life he was a great traveller. He was last
heard of on April 10th 1610, on which day he left England for Venice.

Coningsby's Return
Neen Sollars, Salop. 1606

And when he had risen up the last hill
And could see clearly his parish,
All its teeth and bones, he slipped
From his horse's back and did not walk
But stood very still. His skin showed
The colour of his travels. He wore old
Whiskers and had marks on his arms
From warfare. His horse would go on
So he let it go on, and he was left
Looking through his years of life
At the heart and arteries of England
Which pulsed slowly. *Something*
Is wrong about this country, it is
Too green. Where are the camels
And the itinerant goats? Where
Is the national wisdom? All I see
Are Breughel's cheery bumpkins.
That's not enough. I want sherbet.

The Drinking Boy

From memory I make the clouds
in the pond's water and the elms.

He told me to lie down at the edge,
not to cup my hands but hold my face
almost into the water, as if a thirst
had come on me and all I could do
was drink. The sheep were in the field,
where I had forgotten them. The field
was a heaven they had wandered to.

I lay there, him shouting: *be still boy*,
and I saw the water, full in its face
and the weather's ages pass across it
and my poor figure fall into the soil,
my good boots sold or taken from me
to settle a debt. And I was not paid;
and no heaven for me to pass into.

English Weather

Really quite interesting lights in the sky.
They must have signified something
but at the time we simply stared.

Rainstorms in summer, clouds emptying themselves,
barely a hollow stalk standing in the fields
for Ruth to wander through.

A boy bent to drink from a pool,
not even cupping the water, just
dipping his head in, so thirsty,
letting his sheep wander off.

He is dead now, war or something,
and many of the trees died too,
crumbled into their deep reflections.
The sheep were eaten also.

Only the small boy's innocent thirst
remained: what water was for,
why we have weather.

Pastoral

Always a rogue chainsaw snarling
across sodden down-at-heel fields,
and a dog shouting at travellers,
the yelp of a five-bar gate
being yanked open or slid shut,

and the flashing lamp on the new
item of machinery showing
its return from behind the hill
to the blue corrugated barns
after a day's cultivation,

and the red sunset foreclosing
the unsecured loan of daylight.

The Baby   a Vilanelle

You wake to hear it crying in the night,
The baby that you want but don't have, yet.
Beyond the sleeping world its voice takes flight.

You still don't know its name, one day you might.
It seems to know you though you've not yet met.
You wake to hear it crying in the night.

It will not let you rest, though faint and slight,
It cries the cry of waiting and regret.
Beyond the sleeping world its voice takes flight.

Although your eyes are closed you look for light,
Your mind betrays your flesh, it shouts: you sweat.
You wake to hear it crying in the night.

It's not the skylark singing out of sight.
It's not the moth that flutters round the net.
Beyond the sleeping world its voice takes flight.

The child is dreamed alive, you hold it tight.
You say that you're alright: your face is wet.
You wake to hear it crying in the night.
Beyond the sleeping world its voice takes flight.

Domestic

Having done the washing up
and drying up and the putting away
and having made the sandwiches
and swept the floor and wiped down
the surfaces and loaded the dishwasher
and set it on its nocturnal cycle
and hung up the tea towel,
I have taken myself upstairs
to the attic bedroom hoping
that I might find there
something very important
to write about.

A Short Piece of Choral Music

It's an evening in late March and in the kitchen
I'm listening to a short piece of choral music,
when my son comes in to fetch himself a bowl
of breakfast cereal which, he tells me, helps
with his revision. And another thing, he goes on,
I shouldn't worry about him because he's going
to be fine: exams, work, life, everything, is going
to be fine. That's a relief, I say to myself, thanks,
now I can listen to this music, which turns out
to be just some fancy noise, nothing
compared with a boy's cheerfulness.

Fight in a Chip Shop

Not overly concerned about anything
it seems to me, relentlessly optimistic
despite our best efforts. I keep on thinking

that things may go terribly wrong for you,
but I'm not sure you'd notice, not sure
that you wouldn't simply talk instead about

something extraordinary you'd just seen:
a bird of prey – a red kite – with nothing better
to do than lounge around in the air as if

it owned the place or a Maserati Bora,
accelerating between traffic lights or,
alarmingly, a fight in a chip shop, in which

you report, *two sausages got battered*.

Margaret in the Garden

With your new strappy sandals and summer top
~~and sat~~ *sitting* in the one garden chair against the fence,
with the light breeze lifting the hem of your skirt
and the corners of your Sunday newspaper,
you remind me of one of those domestic landscapes
from between the wars, now so laden with foreboding
that we feel worried when we look at them.

Your tea will be getting cold and a vapour trail
in the blue has disappeared already and the hours
are waiting to be used and if the clouds come over
you'll need a cardigan, and if it rains you'll come
indoors, but for the moment you grace the garden
unthreatened by the weather or the future, holding
the day at arm's length, like you hold the paper.

Are You Off To Sleep?

Are you off to sleep?
Let me know when you get there,
a sign, a text, your breath coming more slowly.

While you're there would you do this for me:
would you look around and make notes,
what dry stone walls, what water butts,
how many orchards and bonfires
and greenhouses you encounter,
things like that?

But you probably won't.
Your sleep will be full of your own
archetypes and patterns and moments
of symmetry; these,
I can't ever know.

But which I want to know.
But which I can't know.

Song

Every night, as they go to bed
and turn off their bedside lamps
and present themselves to sleep,
she says to him, sleepily:
Are you going to sing to me?

No, he replies, *no, I am not,*
but I will recite a short poem.
…
A poem, she says, drowsily,
I'd sooner have a song.

A poem is a song, he says,
but one that does not care
much if you join in or not.
Oh, she says, *well, as long*
as it won't keep me awake.

Poem

I wanted to cross the tidal river
by means of the ford the Romans found
and stumble up the shingle beach
to a new life on the northern shore.

And I wanted to have passed halfway,
midstream, drifting, a man heading south,
taking in water but likely to make it,
his heart set on seeing the turf maze

and buying a drink in the isolated pub.
And I will see him gather up my life
like a number of stacks of small change
stood on the mild- or bitter-puddled table.

Smith/Doorstop Books, Pamphlets and Audio

25 *years*

of titles by

Moniza Alvi, Simon Armitage, Jane Aspinall, Ann Atkinson, Annemarie
Austin, Sally Baker, Mike Barlow, Kate Bass, Suzanne Batty, Chris
Beckett, Peter Bennet, Catherine Benson, Gerard Benson, Sujata Bhatt,
Nina Boyd, Sue Boyle, Susan Bright, Carole Bromley, Sue Butler, Liz
Cashdan, Dennis Casling, Julia Casterton, Clare Chapman, Linda Chase,
Debjani Chatterjee, Chris Considine, Stanley Cook, Bob Cooper, Jennifer
Copley, Paula Cunningham, Simon Currie, Duncan Curry, Peter Daniels,
Jonathan Davidson, Kwame Dawes, Julia Deakin, Steve Dearden, Patricia
Debney, Mike Di Placido, Tim Dooley, Jane Draycott, Carol Ann Duffy,
Sue Dymoke, Nell Farrell, Catherine Fisher, Janet Fisher, Sam Gardiner,
Adele Geras, Sally Goldsmith, Yvonne Green, Harry Guest, Robert
Hamberger, Sophie Hannah, John Harvey, Jo Haslam, Geoff Hattersley,
Jeanette Hattersley, Marko Hautala, Selima Hill, Andrea Holland, Sian
Hughes, Keith Jafrate, Lesley Jeffries, Chris Jones, Mimi Khalvati, John
Killick, Stephen Knight, Judith Lal, John Lancaster, Peter Lane, Michael
Laskey, Brenda Lealman, Tim Liardet, John Lyons, Cheryl Martin, Eleanor
Maxted, John McAuliffe, Michael McCarthy, Patrick McGuinness, Kath
Mckay, Paul McLoughlin, Hugh McMillan, Ian McMillan, Allison McVety,
Hilary Menos, Paul Mills, Hubert Moore, David Morley, Paul Munden, Les
Murray, Dorothy Nimmo, Stephanie Norgate, Christopher North, Carita
Nystrom, Sean O'Brien, Padraig O'Morain, Alan Payne, Pascale Petit, Ann
Pilling, Jim Pollard, Simon Rae, Irene Rawnsley, Ed Reiss, Padraig Rooney,
Jane Routh, Michael Schmidt, Myra Schneider, Ted Schofield, Kathryn
Simmonds, Lemn Sissay, Felicity Skelton, Catherine Smith, Elspeth Smith,
Joan Jobe Smith, Cherry Smyth, Pauline Stainer, Martin Stannard, Adam
Strickson, Mandy Sutter, Diana Syder, Pam Thompson, Susan Utting, Steven
Waling, Martyn Wiley, Andrew Wilson, River Wolton, Sue Wood, Anna
Woodford, Mary Woodward, Cliff Yates ...

www.poetrybusiness.co.uk